I0460244

RAYMOND SMITH

The Greater the Love, The Deeper the Grief

Hope Beyond the Tears

DISCIPLE
BLUEPRINT
PRESS

First edition

ISBN: 979-8-9985686-3-3

This book was professionally typeset on Reedsy.
Find out more at reedsy.com

To Wendy,
My beloved wife and partner for 33 unforgettable years.
Your love was a constant reminder of God's grace, and your faith
was an anchor that steadied my soul. Losing you has been the
hardest journey of my life, but through the tears, I've felt your love
and His presence guiding me.
This book is dedicated to the beautiful legacy you left behind—a
legacy of love, faith, and hope that continues to inspire me every
day.
Until we meet again in eternity, you remain forever in my heart.

Contents

Preface

If you are reading this book, it means you have likely lost someone close to you. I know the journey of grief is never truly over, but I also know that we don't walk it alone. I wrote this prayer because the strength to endure comes from turning to God daily, trusting in His promises, and relying on His unwavering love. My hope is that as you navigate this difficult season, you will experience God's presence in profound ways and find comfort in His eternal promises.

Heavenly Father,

Thank You for Your Son, Jesus Christ, who paid the price for our sins and secured the promise of eternal life. Because of His sacrifice, I have the blessed assurance that one day I will join You in Heaven, reunited with Wendy and my loved ones. Thank You for this gift of grace that transcends all understanding.

Lord, I praise You for who You are—faithful, loving, and true to Your Word. Your promises are unchanging, and because of Your perfect nature, we can trust You completely. Thank You for the hope that anchors our souls, even in the deepest valleys of grief.

I lift up each reader of this book to You. Illuminate Your Word in their hearts, Lord. May it not only be understood but come alive within them, shaping their lives and drawing them closer to You. Let Your Holy Spirit fill them with comfort, strength, and hope. Lead them gently as they navigate the pain and uncertainties of grief. Help them to lean on You and find peace in Your presence.

Father, I pray that You help them to keep their eyes fixed on the prize—the promise of eternity with You in Heaven. Remind them that our time on earth is brief, but eternity is forever. In Your presence, there will be no more pain, tears, or sickness. Let this truth bring hope and encouragement as they walk through their days.

Finally, Lord, I ask that You surround them with Your love and remind them daily that they are not alone. You are with them, carrying them, strengthening them, and leading them toward a future filled with Your promises.

May this journey, though painful, ultimately draw them closer to You. May they experience Your peace that surpasses all understanding and Your joy that is their strength. And may they look forward with anticipation to the day when all things are made new.

In Jesus' name, Amen.

Acknowledgments

Writing this book has been both a journey of grief and healing, and I could not have done it alone. Grief is a journey that will never be complete.

First and foremost, I want to thank my Lord and Savior, Jesus Christ, for walking with me through the darkest valleys and giving me the strength to share this story. Your promises have been my anchor and my hope.

To my daughter Mandy: Your help in taking care of your mom was priceless, and now I look forward to our daily calls and texts. You have helped sustained me in ways I cannot fully express, and I am deeply grateful and very proud of you.

To my son Wes: Thank you for being an inspiration to me! I am very proud of you!

To my cousin Carol, an additional gift I received from marrying Wendy is for you to come into my life. Your encouragement and friendship mean the world to me.

To my brother-in-law Kevin and his wife Kati, your kindness and support have been a lifeline. From the meals you provided to the Sundays spent watching football with me, you have been a source of comfort and joy. I am deeply grateful for your love and presence in my life. Also, thank you for sharing your kids with me.

To my niece Khloe and my nephews Maizon and Owen: You bring me so much joy because you want to spend time with Uncle Raymond. Whether it is driving to church, watching YouTube, going to the movies, or going to lunch after church, you have been a tremendous blessing to me. Khloe, I will never forget the Rattlesnake Roundup.

To my family in Rockwall, Texas. Bob and Bridget Megna and all of your family, your love, support and encouragement and knowing you are always there for me is priceless. Bridget, you helped inspire me to write this book!

To my family and friends, thank you for your unwavering support. To my church family at Hilltop Baptist Church, thank you for your prayers and encouragement during this season of loss.

A special thank you to my Pastor, Max Simms, for your unwavering support and encouragement throughout this journey. Your guidance and prayers have been a blessing, and I am so thankful for your leadership.

To the followers of Disciple Blueprint, your encouragement inspired me to write this book.

Finally, to those who pick up this book: thank you for trusting me with your journey through grief. It is my prayer that these words will bring you comfort, hope, and the assurance of God's presence in every season of life.

1

Chapter 1: Our Story—Faith, Family, and Love

Every great love story begins with a moment—ours began in church. Wendy and I met at Metropolitan Bible Church in Dallas, Texas. We were both walking into a new season, each bringing a child from a previous marriage, and each praying for something more lasting, more centered in Christ. A few months after meeting, we began dating. By month three, I knew. I proposed, and she said yes. Five months later, on November 29, 1991, we were married.

I was a native Texan. Wendy was from Farmers Valley, Pennsylvania—a place I couldn't even point to on a map at the time. But God knew what He was doing. From the beginning, He was blending not only two lives but two families. Before we even exchanged vows, my son had begun calling Wendy "Mom," and her daughter had started calling me "Daddy." It was a holy blending, something only God could orchestrate.

Wendy was a Christian school teacher—later a principal. Teaching was her calling and her gift. Whether speaking to a classroom of teenagers or leading a women's Bible study, she had the rare ability to hold attention and touch hearts. Every lesson was bathed in prayer and backed by preparation. Women flocked to her Sunday School classes because her teaching wasn't surface-level—it was soul-deep.

But it wasn't just teaching. Wendy had the gift of hospitality. Every house we ever lived in became a home—filled with Scripture in every room, warmth in every corner, and always an open door. Our home was a refuge for family, friends, church members, and even the occasional stranger. Wendy made sure of it.

Our life together was centered on four things: faith, family, friends, and work. I spent 44 years in the Information Technology industry, serving in various roles in church as well—youth director, teacher, AWANA commander, deacon, treasurer, and men's ministry leader. We ministered together, prayed together, struggled together, and dreamed together.

One of the greatest tests of our marriage came during the last years of Wendy's mother's life. She was in a nursing home in Smethport, Pennsylvania—1,500 miles from our home in Forney, Texas. Wendy felt called to be near her, so she resigned from her job and moved back to care for her mom. I stayed in Texas to work. It was a year of long-distance sacrifice. That year, we were physically apart for over 75% of the time—but emotionally and spiritually, we were closer than ever. God used even that separation to strengthen our bond.

We were opposites in many ways—she was structured, disciplined, always moving. I was more laid back, unhurried. But we brought out the best in each other. Our differences weren't friction points; they were complementary forces that created a stronger whole.

Through the years, we faced grief, parenting challenges,

ministry hardships, and job stress. But the one thing we never struggled with was our love for each other. It was unconditional, unshakeable.

The last four months of Wendy's life were a testament to that love. She began feeling ill around Thanksgiving 2023. By December 28—my birthday—we received the diagnosis: pancreatic cancer. She battled bravely. There were hospital stays, difficult days, and constant caregiving. Through it all, I watched the woman I loved face unimaginable pain with unimaginable grace.

On April 2, 2024, at 9:30 PM, Wendy went to be with the Lord. That's when my grief journey truly began. But even in the darkness, I could see the light of what God had given me: thirty-three years with a woman whose love transformed me.

Wendy didn't just impact me—she left a legacy. She influenced hundreds of students and parents through her godly approach to education. Her desire wasn't just to teach subjects; it was to lead souls to Christ. Her prayer journals were filled with names—family, friends, students, parents—many of whom never knew they were being lifted to the throne of grace. Even those who caused her difficulty at school became subjects of her most fervent prayers.

She also left a lasting impression on our children. Our daughter Amanda, or Mandy as we call her, witnessed how Wendy ministered to her mother and later mirrored that same devotion when she came to Pennsylvania to care for Wendy during her battle with cancer. I could never repay Mandy for the compassion and strength she showed.

Our story wasn't perfect, but it was purposeful. God wrote it. And now, as I write these pages, I do so to honor Wendy, our journey, and the Savior who held us together.

This is where the story begins—not at Wendy's passing, but in the love that continues to shape my days and guide my steps. The greater the love, the deeper the grief. And through that grief, I've discovered something even deeper: the unshakeable hope we have in Christ and that there is hope beyond the tears.

When I started writing my blog, I played with a poem from one of my posts and I discovered I like writing poetry. It was really something I had never tried before. This poem is about Wendy. You will find a poem at the end of each chapter.

My beautiful Princess! Wendy picking blackberries on the hill!

Wendy, God's Greatest Gift

From the first moment I saw you, I knew,
Our lives were meant to be shared, me and you.
Your golden hair first caught my eye,
But it was your soul that lifted me high.

Sassy and quick, your wit made me grin,
Yet it was your heart that drew me in.
A beauty unmatched, both inside and out,
You taught me what love is truly about.

With gifts from God, you shined so bright,
Teaching with passion, inspiring with might.
From students in classrooms to women you led,
You worked tirelessly, pouring all that you had.

And oh, your gift of hospitality!
Each home you made was filled with tranquility.
Scripture adorned each room with grace,
Welcoming all who entered the space.

We built our dreams, though not all came true,
But each moment we shared, I cherished with you.
I miss your hand, so soft in mine,
A love so pure, eternal, divine.

The smell of coffee still lingers here,

Though I don't drink it, it draws you near.
You needed it to start the day,
Without it, the world might stray.

I miss watching you in your sacred place,
Tending the garden with gentle embrace.
The ducks you cared for, the meals you made,
In all you did, your love never swayed.

A hole now lives where my heart once was whole,
An ache that echoes deep in my soul.
Yet I know one day, in Heaven's glow,
We'll be together, where love will overflow.

Wendy, my love, my life, my best,
In you, I found God's richest bequest.
Until that day when I see you again,
I'll carry your love in my heart till then.

2

Chapter 2: My Journey

April 2, 2024, 9:30 PM—

That moment is seared into my memory. I had just pulled into the airport to pick up my son, Wes, when my daughter called to say, "Dad, she's gone." Wendy had taken her final breath while I was on the road, praying we'd all be able to be there together. Before I left for the airport, I sat by her side, holding her hand as her breathing grew more labored. I kissed her for what would be the last time, whispered that I loved her, and told her she could let go if she needed to. Still, I held out hope that Wes would make it in time. He didn't—but I know Wendy knew he was coming. And I believe she knew how deeply she was loved.

And so began my journey through grief.

The truth is, nothing can prepare you for the emptiness that follows the death of someone you love deeply. No words of comfort, no previous loss, no amount of faith can insulate you from that initial wave of pain. I had been preparing in some ways for months, watching Wendy's body weaken as cancer took its toll. But there's a difference between anticipating a loss and experiencing it. The moment she passed, it wasn't just that she was gone—it was that life as I knew it had fundamentally changed.

The house, once filled with her voice, her routines, her presence, was now painfully silent. The smell of coffee in the morning (which she absolutely needed to function) was gone. So were the little sounds of her in the garden, her ducks quacking as she ushered them into their pen each night, and her feet pacing as she planned women's ministry events. I missed it all. And I still do.

I had heard people say that grief is the price we pay for love. But now I was living it. And the price felt staggering.

It was in those early days that a thought began to echo in my heart: The greater the love, the deeper the grief.

We had a deep love—a God-authored, hard-won, grace-filled kind of love. It was far from perfect, but it was rooted in faith and sustained by years of walking through life hand-in-hand. That's what made the loss so profound.

At first, I tried to be strong. I buried myself in tasks. I cared for the dogs, the ducks, the house. But eventually, the weight of it all broke through. One evening, after putting the ducks in for the night—something Wendy always did—I stood by the pond and sobbed. The ache was too much. The silence too loud. I didn't know how to move forward.

But even in that darkness, God's Word began to speak light.

Psalm 34:18 (NLT) says, "The Lord is close to the broken-hearted; he rescues those whose spirits are crushed." That was me. Crushed. Broken. But not alone. I began to sense His presence in the stillness. Not always with answers—but always with comfort.

I was reminded of Ecclesiastes 3:1–4, which tells us, "For everything there is a season, a time for every activity under heaven... A time to cry and a time to laugh. A time to grieve and a time to dance." I realized I was in a season of mourning, and God wasn't asking me to skip ahead. He was asking me to sit with Him in it.

Some days, I still shouted at God. Other days, I sat in silence. Sometimes, I'd cry without warning. Grief has no timetable. But in each moment, God met me—not with condemnation, but with compassion.

Looking back now, I see that this wasn't just a time of mourning. It was the beginning of transformation. I began to reflect not only on what I had lost, but on what I had been given. Thirty-three years with Wendy. A marriage filled with laughter, love, challenges, and Christ. A partner who pointed me to Jesus daily and loved me unconditionally.

Her passing wasn't the end of our story. It was the continuation of a greater story—God's story.

I don't claim to have mastered grief. It still sneaks up on me and hardly a day passes without tears. Some days are still hard. But I've come to understand that grief is not something to escape or conquer. It's something to walk through—with God.

In this journey, I've discovered that God's promises are not just comforting phrases. They are anchors. They hold me steady when everything else feels unstable. Wendy's life and legacy continue to inspire me daily, and as I share this story, I do so not from a place of having it all figured out, but from a place of hope rooted in faith.

My journey isn't over. But I no longer walk it alone. God is with me, every step. And maybe, just maybe, this journey—my grief journey—will help someone else find their way too.

"The Lord is close to the brokenhearted." I've lived it. And so, friend, can you.

Wendy and her Dogs! Penn, the golden and Riley, the Doodle

In The Quiet of Grief

In the quiet of grief, where echoes dwell,
A story unfolds only the heart can tell.
Love so deep, its roots unshaken,
Leaves an ache when its source is taken.

Chairs left empty, traditions undone,
The light of the past eclipses the sun.
Yet in the shadows, a whisper grows,
A gentle reminder that love still flows.

The greater the love, the deeper the pain,

Yet love's sweet memory will ever remain.
In the songs of the birds, the soft morning hue,
A promise of hope arises anew.

Through garland and stockings, the past appears,
Laced with laughter, now blurred by tears.
But God, in His mercy, meets us there,
With arms of comfort and tender care.

Each cardinal's flight, each flicker of light,
Reminds us He's near, through day and night.
In loss, we find His grace outpoured,
A love eternal, forever assured.

So, sit on the porch, breathe in the air,
Though the chair beside you may be bare.
The presence of love, though unseen, is real,
And through God's embrace, we begin to heal.

In the quiet of grief, where pain may lie,
Faith lifts us up to see the sky.
For even in sorrow, His light breaks through,
And His promises whisper, "I am with you."

3

Chapter 3: When Love Meets Loss

Grief is one of the most profound emotions we can experience. It is not merely an emotional response but a spiritual and physical one as well. When Wendy passed, my world changed. There was no preparation, no real way to brace for the silence that followed her absence. What followed were waves of emotions—sadness, anger, confusion, even moments of numbness. It's in these moments of raw vulnerability that I found myself face to face with the depth of love we shared.

One of the most comforting yet striking verses in Scripture is John 11:35 (NLT): "Then Jesus wept." These three words hold immense power. Jesus, knowing He was about to raise Lazarus from the dead, still paused to grieve. He didn't bypass the moment. He felt the sting of death. He stood in solidarity with those mourning. He wept because His heart broke for Mary, Martha, and the others. But I believe He also wept because He knew I would weep. He entered into our suffering not just to redeem it but to experience it with me. That's a loving and compassionate Savior.

Jesus' decision to pause and grieve teaches us something

profound about the character of God. It shows us that our pain matters to Him. We are not alone in our sorrow. He is present in the quiet sobs, the restless nights, and the empty spaces left by our loved ones. And because of His divine nature, He is able to minister to each of us personally, bringing the comfort only He can provide.

Grief is not a sign of weakness or a lack of faith. It is the evidence of deep love. The greater the love, the deeper the grief. I loved Wendy with every fiber of my being, and losing her has left a void that words fail to describe. But I have come to see that my grief is not something to be ashamed of; it is a reflection of the beautiful life we shared.

Jesus' humanity was on full display at Lazarus' tomb. Though He had divine power, He also had a heart that felt pain. This intersection of divinity and humanity brings hope to our grief. If Jesus, being God, could grieve, so can we. And in our grief, we find that He doesn't rush us through the process. He walks with us in it. There is no set timetable for grief. Some may begin to feel lighter in a few weeks; others, like me, may find that it takes months or even years. And that's okay. God's timeline is not ours. What matters is that we walk the path, however long it may be, with Him.

Ecclesiastes 3:1–4 (NLT) reminds us, "For everything there is a season". Grief comes in seasons, and sometimes those seasons align with the calendar. For me, the time from Thanksgiving to Christmas was especially hard. It included our anniversary and countless traditions that Wendy and I cherished. I couldn't decorate the house for Christmas. I didn't want to pretend everything was okay. But God was gracious and patient. He allowed me space to grieve while gently reminding me of His presence.

Through grief, God invites us into deeper relationship with Him. My morning times with God became my anchor. In the silence, I heard His voice. In the loneliness, I felt His companionship. In the darkness, His promises shined the brightest. What had once been a quiet house became a sanctuary, a holy space where I met with the One who never leaves or forsakes.

I've learned that silence can be both an enemy and a friend. If I allow the enemy to fill the silence, he will whisper lies—that I'm alone, that God is unfair, that there's no purpose in the pain. But if I invite God into the silence, I hear truth. I hear Him say, "I am with you." I hear reminders of His faithfulness, His love, and His promises. The key is choosing who I sit with in the silence.

The story of Wendy's life, our love, and my grief has become part of my testimony. It's a sacred story—one marked by tears, but also by grace. As I continue walking this path, I do so with the assurance that Jesus walks with me. He knows my pain, and He grieves with me. But He also brings hope. And in that hope, I find strength to take the next step.

As Queen Elizabeth II once said, "Grief is the price we pay for love." If your grief runs deep, it means your love was strong. And in that love, and in your grief, Jesus stands beside you, weeping with you—and walking with you toward healing.

Throughout this book, I've shared stories from my journey through grief—some heavy, some hopeful, all honest. But I also recognize that your journey may look different from mine. That's why at the end of Chapters 3 through 10, you'll find a section called **"Going Deeper."** These were created to give you space to pause, reflect, and personally engage with the themes in each chapter. Each one includes Scripture, prayer, and questions designed to help you walk more closely with God through your own season of sorrow. My prayer is that these moments of reflection will draw you nearer to the One who walks with us through the valley—and who leads us toward hope.

Going Deeper

Grief is not something we just read about—it's something we live through. While the chapter you just read shares part of my journey, I know that your experience with grief is personal and unique. This section is here to help you slow down, reflect, and engage with God more intentionally as you walk through your own healing. My prayer is that these questions, scriptures, and practices draw you closer to the One who weeps with us—and gives us hope beyond the tears.

Scripture Focus:

John 11:35 (NLT) — "Then Jesus wept."

Even though Jesus knew He would raise Lazarus, He chose to weep with those who were mourning. His tears validated the pain of grief and remind us that God meets us in our sorrow.

Reflection Questions:

- What does it mean to you that Jesus wept?
- How does it feel to know that God understands and shares in your grief?
- Are there moments you've felt like no one understood your pain? How might this passage offer a new perspective?

Prayer Prompt:

Lord, thank You for being a Savior who weeps. Thank You for entering into our sorrow instead of avoiding it. Help me feel Your presence in my pain and give me the courage to be honest with You in my grief. Amen.

Spiritual Practice:

Spend ten minutes in silence today. As thoughts arise, picture Jesus sitting beside you—not to speak, but simply to be with you. Let His presence comfort you, even in the quiet.

Our family, left to right, Wes, Wendy, Me and Mandy!

Why Jesus Wept

He stood before the tomb that day,
Where sorrow's weight in silence lay.
Though He knew His power to heal,
Still, the depth of love He couldn't conceal.

He saw the tears, He heard the cries,
Compassion welled within His eyes.
Not just the death, but the pain it bore,
Drove His heart to weep once more.

Jesus wept, for love so pure,
Grief and loss He, too, endured.
In those tears, divinity shone,
A God who weeps, yet never alone.

If He could grieve, so can we,
For love's deep roots, grief must decree.
But in His tears, there's hope to find,
A Savior's love, so intertwined.

So when your sorrow seems too great,
Remember Jesus, who faced this weight.
He wept for love, He wept for pain,
And through those tears, we find our gain.

4

Chapter 4: Feeling His Presence

Grief has a way of isolating us. It can make the world feel like it's spinning while we stand still, locked in a space where silence becomes deafening. But I've learned that silence is not always the enemy—it's what we do with the silence that makes all the difference. When grief silences the world around us, it creates a space where we either lean into God or allow the enemy to gain a foothold.

In those early days after Wendy passed, silence surrounded me. The chatter of our day-to-day life disappeared, and with it came an overwhelming void. Satan used that silence to whisper lies into my heart—lies that God was distant, that He had forgotten me, that He was somehow to blame. It's in these quiet moments that the enemy's voice often grows loudest. He seeks to separate us from God by convincing us that our grief is evidence of abandonment. But the truth is just the opposite. God is especially near to the brokenhearted.

It's why being connected to a church body is so important. Isolation can make us vulnerable, but community brings strength. Even though I was surrounded by people who loved me, the grief still settled heavily in my heart. And still, it was in the quiet that God's presence gently met me.

I've had two profound experiences where God met me in grief. The first was when I lost my sister, Saundra. She had been thrown from a horse and sustained a fatal brain injury. After weeks in the hospital, we were told she was brain-dead. I was devastated and angry. I remember going into the small chapel at the hospital and pouring out my anger at God, why didn't He take her when the accident happened. Why did she have to lie in a hospital for weeks. I didn't hold anything back. Later, a nurse told me they heard me in the ICU. But in that stillness afterward, the Holy Spirit impressed upon me something profound: our family wasn't ready to lose her earlier. That simple thought brought peace and helped me to move forward.

This experience laid a foundation for when Wendy passed. The grief felt deeper, the silence heavier. Once again, I found myself crying out to God, filled with anger and pain. I asked Him why. Why her? Why now? Why not me instead? As I poured out my sorrow, the Holy Spirit whispered a question into my heart: "What if Jesus had asked the Father why He had to die for your sins?" That stopped me cold. It reframed everything. Jesus surrendered to death not because I deserved it but because of His love. That realization transformed my anger into praise.

God wants us to be real with Him. He wants authenticity, not religious performance. David, in the Psalms, shows us this over and over. Psalm 62:8 (NLT) says, "O my people, trust in him at all times. Pour out your heart to him, for God is our refuge." And in Psalm 34:18 (NLT), we're reminded, "The Lord is close to the brokenhearted; he rescues those whose spirits are crushed."

Silence isn't the enemy. It's what we do in the silence that matters. For me, the silence of my home slowly became a sacred space. I'd sit on my porch and listen—not just to the wind or the distant sounds of children playing—but for God. And I began to hear Him in those still moments. In the chirping of birds, the rustling of leaves, and the memories of Wendy that flooded my heart.

But not all silence is healthy. Many people try to avoid it by staying constantly busy—filling their schedules to avoid facing their pain. That's just postponing the inevitable. Real healing happens when we stop and sit with the silence, when we allow God to meet us there.

One of the most emotionally difficult moments in my grief journey came the day after Wendy's Celebration of Life service in Pennsylvania. It was a Saturday when we honored her memory, and the following morning, my daughter Mandy—who had been by my side for four months—left to return home. As we said our goodbyes, I tried to prepare myself for church, but something inside me was unraveling.

During Sunday School, I wept quietly, but by the time I reached the worship service, the tears wouldn't stop. I had to get up and leave during the middle of the service. I was overwhelmed with sorrow. I knew what awaited me when I got home—an empty house. For the first time in this journey, I felt completely abandoned. It was, without a doubt, the lowest point I had experienced since Wendy's passing.

That same day was my niece Khloe's birthday. I love that little girl deeply, and under normal circumstances, nothing would have kept me from celebrating with her. But I simply couldn't do it. The idea of being around anyone felt impossible. I sat alone in my quiet house, and then on my front porch, letting the weight of grief settle in.

As I sat there, the stillness turned into a battlefield. My

emotions darkened, and anger began to build. I realized I was allowing Satan to speak into the silence, planting lies and feeding despair. But something stirred in me—I knew I couldn't stay in that place. I went inside and turned on a sermon from Lakepointe Church in Rockwall, Texas on YouTube. I don't even remember what the sermon was about. As the Word of God was preached, it was as if light poured into the darkness. Satan fled, and in that moment, something shifted. Hope—small and fragile—began to take root again.

In that silence, I chose to let God in.

If you're in the middle of grief, don't fear the silence. Embrace it. Pour out your heart to God. Let Him meet you in that quiet place. He is not far. He is near. He's not put off by your questions or anger. He's big enough to handle them and gracious enough to answer in ways that transform our pain into peace.

Going Deeper

Loneliness often arrives quietly—especially in grief. It slips in after the funeral or Celebration of Life, after the meals stop coming, after the calls slow down. This chapter focused on how God's presence doesn't vanish when people fade away. He is near in the silence, in the stillness, and even in the ache. This section will help you reflect more intentionally on what it means to experience God's presence when the world feels empty—and how to invite Him into the loneliness.

Scripture Focus:

Psalm 34:18 (NLT) — "The Lord is close to the brokenhearted;

he rescues those whose spirits are crushed."

In moments of overwhelming loneliness, this verse reminds us that God's presence is not distant. He draws especially near when our hearts are broken.

Reflection Questions:

- In what ways have you experienced God's presence during your grief?
- When have you felt most alone in this journey?
- What would it look like to invite God into that loneliness today?

Prayer Prompt:

Father, I feel the ache of absence and the weight of silence. But Your Word says You are close to the brokenhearted. Help me to sense Your nearness in the quiet moments. Open my heart to feel Your love, even when I cannot see or hear You clearly. Amen.

Spiritual Practice:

Set aside five minutes to sit in stillness. Before you begin, pray, "Lord, I'm here. Please meet me here." Focus on your breathing and imagine God's presence surrounding you. If you're comfortable, end the time by writing a short prayer or letter to Him expressing what you're feeling today.

Mandy and Wendy! Don't I have beautiful ladies!

Through the Darkness to Light

In the shadow of despair, I knelt alone,
The weight of grief, a heart of stone.
Questions echoed, "Why, O Lord, why?"
Tears fell fast, as storms raged in the sky.

The silence deafened, no voice to hear,
Loneliness whispered, fed every fear.
The cross seemed distant, a dim-lit flame,
I cried out, trembling, calling His name.

But then, a glimmer, faint and small,

25

A ray of hope began to call.
A gentle voice, not loud, but clear,
"I am with you; I'm always near."

Through the kindness of a friend's embrace,
In every call, in every face.
The storm still raged, but light broke through,
A reminder: "I will carry you."

The cross now shines, a radiant glow,
His love sustains, this I know.
From brokenness, beauty takes its place,
Grief turns to hope through His boundless grace.

So take heart, dear soul, the night won't stay,
The dawn is coming; He'll light your way.
Through the darkest valleys, He walks beside,
Your pain, your tears, He will not hide.

5

Chapter 5: Finding Strength in Surrender

Grief invites an endless stream of questions, most of them beginning with a single word: Why? Why Wendy? Why did she have to suffer? Why now? Why not me instead? These questions consumed my thoughts, fueled my anxiety, and created a growing wall between me and God. I lost sleep. I began to binge eat. I could feel the emotional pressure mounting within me. And, truthfully, I didn't initially want relief. Sitting in my sorrow, clinging to my grief, almost felt like the only thing I could do. Without responsibilities—my job, the dogs, and Wendy's ducks—I might have completely shut down. But those daily obligations pulled me forward, even when I didn't feel ready to move.

It was during one of those dark moments that I had a deeply personal and unforgettable encounter with God. In a desperate outcry, I demanded answers, screamed into the silence, and let loose my frustration and pain. Then, in the stillness that followed, the Holy Spirit asked a question that changed everything: "What if Jesus had asked why He had to die for your sins?"

The weight of that realization brought me to my knees. Jesus, sinless and perfect, didn't deserve the agony of the cross. He didn't deserve to be mocked, beaten, and crucified. Yet He surrendered—willingly, humbly, fully. And He did it for me. The contrast was staggering. I was clinging to my questions, unwilling to let go, while Jesus had already surrendered for me. In that moment, I understood: if He could surrender for my eternal salvation, then I could surrender to Him in my grief.

Isaiah 55:8–9 (NLT) tells us, "'My thoughts are nothing like your thoughts,' says the Lord. 'And my ways are far beyond anything you could imagine. For just as the heavens are higher than the earth, so my ways are higher than your ways and my thoughts higher than your thoughts.'"

These verses were the last thing I wanted to hear early in my grief. I didn't want to be reminded that I wouldn't get answers. I wanted understanding, not trust. But through time and prayer, my perspective began to shift. I realized that God sees not just my present pain, but the entire arc of my life—past, present, and future. I only see the broken pieces. He sees the masterpiece.

When we trust that God's ways are higher, we begin to loosen our grip on the need for answers. We may not know why something happened, but we can know Who holds it all together. That truth became a cornerstone of my healing.

The Jonah Reminder: Surrender Is Daily

One of the clearest biblical examples of resistance to God's plan is found in the story of Jonah. Jonah had a direct command from God, but he ran the other way. He didn't want to go to Nineveh. He didn't want to preach repentance to people he despised. His refusal led him into the belly of a great fish—a place of confinement, reflection, and ultimately, surrender.

Jonah's story reminds us that surrender is not a one-time

event. Even after being delivered, Jonah continued to wrestle with God's plan. How often are we like Jonah—knowing what God wants but resisting because it doesn't align with our expectations? Grief is a daily battle, and so is surrender. Some days, it's easy. Other days, it takes everything we have.

"Trust in the Lord with all your heart; do not depend on your own understanding. Seek his will in all you do, and he will show you which path to take." —Proverbs 3:5–6 (NLT)

These verses became my roadmap when I didn't know which way to turn. Trusting God with all your heart doesn't mean you won't still hurt. It means that, even in the hurt, you choose to believe He is working. That He is guiding. That He is holding you together.

How to Practice This Kind of Trust:

- Start with honesty: Tell God exactly how you feel. He can handle your pain.
- Lean on Scripture: Let His promises replace your questions.
- Pause before reacting: In moments of anger or despair, stop and pray.
- Look for His fingerprints: Notice the small moments when He shows up.

"Then Jesus said, 'Come to me, all of you who are weary and carry heavy burdens, and I will give you rest. Take my yoke upon you. Let me teach you, because I am humble and gentle at heart, and you will find rest for your souls.'" —Matthew 11:28–29 (NLT)

I was weary. My soul felt crushed under the weight of loss. And this invitation from Jesus felt like water in the desert. To surrender is not to give up—it is to give over. We hand our burdens to the One who can carry them.

The night before His crucifixion, Jesus prayed in the Garden of Gethsemane. He was fully God, but also fully man. He felt the weight of what was coming—the betrayal, the beatings, the humiliation, and the cross. He prayed, "My Father! If it is possible, let this cup of suffering be taken away from me. Yet I want your will to be done, not mine" (Matthew 26:39 (NLT).

Can we pause here and sit in the gravity of that moment? Jesus didn't want the suffering. He didn't want the cross. But He chose it. He surrendered not because it was easy but because it was necessary. His act of surrender wasn't abstract—it was personal. He surrendered for me. He surrendered for you. His obedience in suffering became the pathway to our salvation.

When I reflect on my own questions—the anger, the pleas for understanding—I'm brought back to the garden. If Jesus, in His perfection, could surrender for my redemption, surely I can surrender my grief to the One who gave everything for me.

"Do not be afraid or discouraged, for the Lord will personally go ahead of you. He will be with you; he will neither fail you nor abandon you." —Deuteronomy 31:8 (NLT)

God doesn't just walk with us—He goes ahead of us. That truth became very real to me during the holiday season. Thanksgiving, Christmas, and our anniversary—all within weeks of each other—loomed like mountains I wasn't ready to climb. But God prepared the way. He filled my house with family. He placed it on my heart to spend time with my niece and nephews. He gave me the courage to face what I feared. And every step of the way, He walked before me.

During our marriage, I'd occasionally have dreams where Wendy left me for someone else. It became a joke between us. I'd wake up upset, and she'd smile and say, "So I left you again?"

We'd laugh, because we both knew she never would.

After she passed, the dreams returned—this time with intensity. They weren't funny anymore. I'd wake up feeling betrayed and heartbroken. Some nights I stayed up just to avoid going back to sleep. The dreams were relentless.

One night, in desperation, I thought about Peter walking on the water toward Jesus. Peter was fine until he took his eyes off Christ. When he began to sink, I imagine his prayer was simple but urgent: "Jesus, help me!"

That became my prayer. "Jesus, help me."

I surrendered even my sleep to Him. And the dreams began to fade. On the nights they returned, so did my prayer. "Jesus, help me." And He always does.

At the heart of every question is a longing—for peace, for understanding, for purpose. But the true answer to all our whys isn't found in explanation. It's found in surrender. We surrender because we trust the One who sees the full picture. We surrender because Jesus surrendered for us.

This isn't a one-time decision. It's a daily choice, sometimes an hourly one. But each act of surrender leads us closer to peace, to healing, to hope.

A Final Challenge: Take time today to identify the thing you're struggling to surrender. Is it a question? A fear? A regret? Write it down. Pray over it. And ask Jesus to help you lay it at His feet.

Because the answer to every "why" is this: God has a plan. And His plan is always better than mine.

Going Deeper

Surrender isn't natural when you're grieving. We want answers. We want control. We want to hold tightly to what we've lost. But surrender is where healing begins. In this chapter, I shared how letting go of the "why" questions opened the door to rest and peace. This section is designed to help you think through what surrender looks like in your own grief—how it's not a sign of weakness, but an act of trust in a God who sees the full picture.

Scripture Focus:

Matthew 11:28–29 (NLT) — "Come to me, all of you who are weary and carry heavy burdens, and I will give you rest. Take my yoke upon you. Let me teach you, because I am humble and gentle at heart, and you will find rest for your souls."

Surrender isn't giving up—it's giving over. In this promise, Jesus reminds us that true rest is found when we stop trying to carry grief alone.

Reflection Questions:

- What burdens are you still carrying in your own strength?
- What does surrender look like for you in this season?
- Can you identify any areas where you're resisting God's invitation to rest?

Prayer Prompt:
Lord, I'm tired. I've tried to carry my grief and control the

pieces of my life that feel shattered. But I know You're calling me to rest—to trust—to surrender. Teach me how to release what I can't carry, and help me trust that You'll meet me there. Amen.

Spiritual Practice:

Take a blank piece of paper and write down anything you're holding onto—questions, fears, control, guilt. Fold the paper, hold it in your hands, and pray over it. Then place it in your Bible at Matthew 11:28 as a symbol of surrendering it to God.

Christmas 2023, our last together. Christmas was Wendy's favorite time of year!

Through the Storm, He Holds Me

When the waves crash and the night grows cold,
I cry out to Him, my burdens unfold.
The weight of grief, too much to bear,
In the raging storm, I find Him there.

Heavy chains of sorrow, tightly wound,
My cries of "Why, Lord?" echo around.
Dreams haunt me with a pain so deep,
Yet His promise whispers, "I'm here; don't weep."

His gentle voice cuts through my despair,
"Come to Me, weary one, lay it there.
For My yoke is easy, My burden light,
Find rest in Me through the darkest night."

A text, a call, a kind embrace,
He shows His love in the simplest place.
Through people's hands, His work is done,
In my grief, His light has shone.

The storm still roars, but I'm not alone,
He holds my heart, flesh, and bone.
Through surrender, I find strength anew,
His grace sustains; His love is true.

6

Chapter 6: God Comforts Us to Comfort Others

One of the greatest blessings that can come from grief is the opportunity to extend the same comfort we've received to others. As we've journeyed through the silence, the surrender, and the sorrow, we've also found the presence of God—and in His presence, we've been comforted. But that comfort is not meant to be kept to ourselves. As 2 Corinthians 1:3–4 (NLT) reminds us: "All praise to God, the Father of our Lord Jesus Christ. God is our merciful Father and the source of all comfort. He comforts us in all our troubles so that we can comfort others."

God often places us in situations not only for our growth but also so that we can walk with others on their own journeys of healing. I've come to realize that grief becomes a powerful part of our testimony. Just like someone who's overcome addiction can reach another addict in a way no one else can, someone who has lost a spouse can speak into the life of another grieving spouse with a compassion and clarity that only comes from shared experience.

In my own life, there have been a few key moments that

shaped how I understand this. Wendy and I both went through divorces before God brought us together. While I wouldn't wish divorce on anyone, it became part of our testimony. I remember one couple who came to us struggling to keep their marriage together. Because Wendy and I had been through the pain of divorce and knew what it meant to find healing, we were able to speak truth into their lives. Today, that couple is still together. Our pain gave us a platform to minister to others.

The same is true with grief. When Wendy passed, I was overwhelmed with love and support. Cards, calls, meals, and text messages poured in. My church family, my pastor, my friends, and my relatives surrounded me. Some offered words of encouragement, some sat with me in silence, and some shared their own experiences. That comfort helped my heart begin to heal.

But one moment, in particular, stands out—and it speaks to how God's comfort often comes in unexpected ways. In the summer of 2023, Wendy convinced me to get ducks. We have two small ponds on our property, and while the ducks were originally her idea, she handled all their care. That was our agreement. She could get ducks if I didn't have any responsibility for them. But when she got sick, that responsibility shifted to me. It became part of my daily rhythm—even on bitterly cold mornings when I had to break the ice in the pond so the ducks could swim.

About a month after Wendy passed, I went to the pond to put the ducks away and found myself overwhelmed with emotion. I broke down, sobbing in the quiet of the evening, grieving not only her loss but the quiet, daily routines we once shared. At that very moment, my phone rang. It was my sister-in-law, but when I answered, it was my 11-year-old niece, Khloe, on the line. She had gone to her first dance and spilled soda on her dress. Embarrassed, she asked her mom to pick her up. On the ride home, she asked if I was at home—when her mom said yes, Khloe said, "I need an Uncle Raymond hug."

I told her I was at the pond. What she didn't know was that I desperately needed a Khloe hug. God knew we both needed each other that night. That simple phone call, that small act of love, brought more comfort to my heart than I could have never imagined. Sometimes, comfort doesn't come with grand gestures—it comes in the form of an 11-year-old girl who just wants to hug her uncle.

God doesn't waste our pain. Through our grief, He gives us the ability to bless others. Romans 12:15 (NLT) tells us to "Be happy with those who are happy, and weep with those who weep." This shared experience of sorrow binds us together in powerful ways. When we allow God to use our stories, our brokenness becomes a bridge to someone else's healing.

The peace and comfort that God offers is unlike anything the world can give. Jesus said in John 14:27 (NLT), "I am leaving you with a gift—peace of mind and heart. And the peace I give is a gift the world cannot give. So don't be troubled or afraid." It's this kind of peace that sustained me when nothing else could. People can offer sympathy, but only Christ offers soul-deep peace that transcends understanding.

Isaiah 61:3 (NLT) speaks of giving "a crown of beauty for ashes, a joyous blessing instead of mourning, festive praise instead of despair." That's the God we serve—one who takes our grief and transforms it into something beautiful. And part of that beauty is found when we comfort others.

Here are some practical ways we can offer comfort to others who are grieving:

- Be Present: Sometimes the most meaningful thing you can do is simply show up.
- Listen More Than You Speak: You don't have to fix it. Just be there.
- Share Your Story: Your experience can be a source of healing.
- Offer Help Without Asking: Grievers often don't know what they need—just do it.
- Pray for Them and With Them: Let them hear you speak their name to God.

God will use our stories—if we let Him. When we receive comfort, it's not the end of the journey. It's the beginning of a new calling: to walk alongside others, to share our hope, and to reflect the love and presence of Christ.

In grief, we find God. In comfort, we find purpose. And in sharing, we find joy. That's how God comforts us to comfort others.

Going Deeper

One of the surprising truths about grief is that even in the depth of our pain, God can use us to bring comfort to others. This chapter explored how our testimony—our honest, messy, lived-out story—can become a source of healing for someone else. God never wastes our suffering. This section invites you to reflect on the ways you've been comforted, and how you might begin offering that same comfort to others.

Scripture Focus:

2 Corinthians 1:3–4 (NLT) — "All praise to God, the Father of our Lord Jesus Christ. God is our merciful Father and the source of all comfort. He comforts us in all our troubles so that we can comfort others."

God doesn't just comfort us for our sake—He comforts us so that our story might become someone else's hope.

Reflection Questions:

- Who has been a source of comfort to you during your grief? How did they help you feel seen and loved?
- In what ways might God be calling you to comfort someone else—even if you don't feel fully healed?
- What parts of your story might encourage others walking a similar path?

Prayer Prompt:

Father, thank You for meeting me in my sorrow. Help me not to hide the comfort You've given me but to share it with others who need it. Open my eyes to people around me who are hurting and give me the courage to reach out with empathy and grace. Amen.

Spiritual Practice:

Write down the name of one person you know who may be walking through grief or hardship. Pray for them today, and if you feel led, send them a message or share a short piece of your story as an encouragement.

Khloe and me at the pond. Isn't she beautiful!

In Comfort, We Find Strength

When grief wraps tightly, a shadowed embrace,
And sorrow lingers, leaving no trace.
God whispers gently, "You're not alone,
In My arms, your heart finds its home."

Through every tear, He sends us light,
A friend, a word, to break the night.
A hug, a call, a simple deed,
In our pain, He meets our need.

Yet comfort's gift isn't just for one,
It's a flame to share, like the rising sun.
We are His hands, His voice, His care,
To lift the grieving, to show we're there.

So let your heart extend the grace,
To touch another in their darkened place.
For God's love flows, unbroken and true,
Through comfort shared, He strengthens you.

This poem was not written about Wendy, but my niece Khloe.
The picture above was from that night. I shared the story in this
chapter, but this is one of my favorite poems.

Saved by a Call, Blessed by Her Love

By the pond, I stood in despair,
Grief and sorrow filled the air.
Wendy was gone, her laughter stilled,
A void so vast, it couldn't be filled.

The ducks swam gently, unaware,
Of the weight I bore, the cross I'd wear.
Tears fell freely, my heart undone,
The battle of grief was far from won.

Then a chime—my phone rang near,
A voice so sweet, a lifeline clear.
"Uncle Raymond, I need you now,
A spill on my dress, I don't know how!"

Her words broke through the darkest night,
A spark of love, a guiding light.
She thought she needed my embrace,
But her call brought me saving grace.

I dried my tears, my heart restored,
Her innocent love, my greatest reward.
A spilled soda, a dress in distress,
Became a moment of God's caress.

For in her need, I found my way,
Her laughter chased the dark away.
She was my angel, sent from above,
A reminder of God's unending love.

So now I know, as I always will,
Her call that night, her voice so still,
Was more than a niece reaching out to me,
It was a blessing, setting my spirit free.

7

Chapter 7 - Holding On to Eternal Hope

Many people have written books on grief. Depending on who you read, there are either five stages or seven stages of grief. The five stages include: 1) Denial, 2) Anger, 3) Bargaining, 4) Depression, and 5) Acceptance. The seven stages expand on this: 1) Shock and Denial, 2) Pain and Guilt, 3) Anger and Bargaining, 4) Depression, Reflection, and Loneliness, 5) The Upward Turn, 6) Reconstruction and Recovery, and 7) Acceptance.

Now, a little over a year removed from Wendy's passing, I've had time to reflect on these stages. I never experienced denial or shock—I lived it. For four months, I watched Wendy waste away, unable to eat or drink. Anger? Yes, as we've discussed in earlier chapters, I had moments of anger, but bargaining wasn't part of my journey. Depression was fleeting, lasting perhaps an hour or two at most. Reflection, on the other hand, was significant. During that time, God began changing my perspective. Instead of dwelling on what I lost, I started focusing on what I had. Loneliness was inevitable—after 33 years of being almost always together, the silence was deafening.

What gave me hope, however, was the knowledge that grief is

not the end of the story. As Christians, we have a hope that goes far beyond this life. Our grief is met with God's promises, and those promises remind us that there is more to come. The Bible says that our lives on earth are like a mist—brief and fleeting. When you consider our 60 to 90 years here in comparison to eternity, the brevity of this life pales in comparison. Passages like Revelation 21:4 (NLT), which promises, "He will wipe every tear from their eyes, and there will be no more death or sorrow or crying or pain. All these things are gone forever," and 1 Thessalonians 4:13-18 (NLT), which assures us of the hope of resurrection, brought me profound hope and comfort. These verses became an anchor for my soul, reminding me that grief is temporary, but God's promises are eternal.

Grief, no matter how deep, forces us to confront the reality of loss. Acceptance isn't about forgetting or "moving on" in the sense of leaving someone behind. Rather, it's about coming to terms with the fact that life as we knew it has changed. For me, acceptance began when I started focusing on God's promises instead of my pain. Verses like Revelation 21:4 reminded me that Wendy's suffering had ended and that she was experiencing the fullness of joy in the presence of Christ. 1 Thessalonians 4:13-18 assured me that this separation was only temporary. These scriptures shifted my perspective from the sorrow of my temporary loss to the eternal hope of being reunited in heaven.

God's promises provided a foundation for acceptance by reminding me that He is faithful and unchanging. Psalm 34:18 (NLT) says, "The Lord is close to the brokenhearted; He rescues those whose spirits are crushed." In my most crushed moments, I found God drawing closer, holding me steady. While the grief was deep, the hope of eternity was greater. This eternal perspective allowed me to see beyond the pain and focus on the assurance of God's Word. Reflecting on these truths helped me take the first steps toward acceptance.

Acceptance also came when I reflected on the incredible impact Wendy had on those around her. Her life was a testament to God's love and grace. As a teacher, she poured herself into her students and their families, always pointing them to Christ. One former student sent me a card that simply said, "She changed the course of my life." Her prayer journals, filled with names of people she prayed would come to salvation, were evidence of her servant's heart. Even in her suffering, Wendy left a legacy of faith, love, and selflessness. Reflecting on this legacy didn't erase my grief, but it helped me see how God used her life—and even her passing—for His glory.

Wendy's life reminded me that our purpose as Christians is not only to live for Christ but also to leave a legacy that points others to Him. Her impact on others continues to inspire me each day. God used her to touch lives, and now, I pray He uses me in the same way.

Acceptance isn't the final stage. Grief doesn't end; it evolves. Moving forward doesn't mean leaving your loved one behind—it means continuing your journey with the hope that God has placed before you. For me, moving forward has meant focusing on what lies ahead. It has meant leaning into the promises of Scripture, like James 4:14 (NLT), which says, "How do you know what your life will be like tomorrow? Your life is like the morning fog—it's here a little while, then it's gone."

When I think about the vastness of eternity, I realize just how brief our time on earth truly is. While the pain of Wendy's absence is real, it is temporary. Eternity, on the other hand, is forever. Revelation 21:4 assures us that one day, there will be no more tears, no more pain, and no more separation. This truth gives me strength to face each day, knowing that our time apart is just a moment compared to the endless joy of being together in God's presence.

Moving forward also involves trusting God with the unanswered questions. While I may never fully understand why Wendy's life ended when it did, I trust that God sees the bigger picture. As Isaiah 55:8-9 (NLT) reminds us, "'My thoughts are nothing like your thoughts,' says the Lord. 'And my ways are far beyond anything you could imagine.'" God's plans are higher than ours, and His purposes are always good. This trust has allowed me to take small steps forward, even on the hardest days.

God's promises are not just a comfort; they are a call to action. Moving forward means living with purpose, knowing that our lives have eternal significance. It means embracing each day as an opportunity to reflect His love and hope to a hurting world.

And here's something I remind myself often: If you woke up this morning, God's not done with you yet. No matter your age, background, or season of life, you still have a purpose. God still has work for you to do. Whether it's a word of encouragement, a phone call to someone who is struggling, or simply living your faith authentically, every day is a chance to be the hands and feet of Jesus. Hope in eternity should fuel purpose in the present.

As I've walked through this grief journey, I've come to realize that hope isn't found in forgetting or ignoring the pain. It's found in clinging to God's promises. It's found in remembering the love and legacy of those we've lost and in looking ahead to the joy of eternity. The path to acceptance and moving forward is marked by faith, reflection, and a steadfast trust in the One who holds our future.

If you're in the midst of grief, I encourage you to focus on the promises of Scripture. Meditate on verses like Revelation 21:4 and 1 Thessalonians 4:13-18. Reflect on the legacy of your loved one and how their life pointed to God's glory. And remember that while this life is brief, eternity is forever. Hold on to that hope, for it is the anchor of our souls and the light that guides us through the darkest nights. Embrace the truth that God's promises are not just for the future—they are for today, giving us strength to face each moment with courage and faith.

As Corrie Ten Boom once said, "Never be afraid to trust an unknown future to a known God." Let that truth carry you—through the tears, through the pain, and toward the hope that never fades.

Going Deeper

Grief often narrows our vision. We focus on what we've lost, the empty chair, the silence in the house, the dreams left unfinished. But when we lift our eyes beyond the present pain, we find something far greater waiting—eternal hope. This chapter pointed us toward the promises of heaven, a future with no more tears, no more pain, no more death. Let this section help you reflect on what it means to truly anchor your heart in eternity, even while navigating today's sorrow.

Scripture Focus:

Revelation 21:4 (NLT) — "He will wipe every tear from their eyes, and there will be no more death or sorrow or crying or pain. All these things are gone forever."

This isn't just poetic language—it's a promise from God about the world to come. A world where grief will never touch us again.

Reflection Questions:

- What emotions stir in you when you think about heaven?
- How does the promise of eternity shape your perspective on your current grief?
- Are there ways you can remind yourself daily that your story—and your loved one's—isn't over?

Prayer Prompt:

Lord, thank You for the promise of eternal life through Jesus. Some days it's hard to see beyond my sorrow, but I believe there is more than this. Anchor my heart in eternity. Help me find strength in the assurance that this pain is temporary—and that joy will last forever. Amen.

Spiritual Practice:

Take a few moments today to imagine what heaven might be like—not just streets of gold or beauty beyond comprehension, but the joy of reunion, the absence of grief, the presence of Jesus. Journal what you look forward to most about that day.

At a Christmas Village in Arlington, Texas

Eternal Hope: A Poem of Faith and Healing

When tears flow and hearts ache,
In grief's shadow, we may break.
Yet, through the darkness, a light will shine,
A promise eternal, divine design.

Revelation whispers, "No more pain,"
In Christ, the lost are found again.
Wendy's journey was not in vain,
Her healing came beyond life's chain.

Though we prayed, and hoped for peace,

In heaven, her joy will never cease.
No sorrow, no tears, just heavenly rest,
With God, she dwells, forever blessed.

Grief may linger, but faith will stay,
Guiding us on the narrow way.
For life on earth is but a breath,
Our hope eternal transcends death.

So hold on to His promises true,
In Christ, there's healing for me and you.
With every trial, trust and believe,
God's eternal plan, we'll soon perceive.

8

Chapter 8: Hope in the Resurrection

Grief has a way of isolating us. Even when we are surrounded by people, it can feel as though we're walking alone through a heavy fog. That feeling—emptiness, disconnection, aching separation—is loneliness. It creeps in during the quiet moments, during meals alone, during holidays, during the times when laughter used to fill the air but now is replaced with stillness. For me, grief brought with it an overwhelming sense of being cut off from the life I had always known. It felt like I was wandering without a compass, trying to make sense of a world that no longer included Wendy.

But even in that lonely space, I found hope—real, lasting hope. And it wasn't rooted in wishful thinking. It was grounded in the resurrection of Jesus Christ.

I often think about how lonely Christ must have felt on the cross. He had spent three years pouring His life into others—healing, teaching, discipling. But in His greatest hour of need, His closest friends fled. Peter denied Him. Judas betrayed Him. The rest scattered in fear. And then came the moment that brings me to my knees: the moment when God the Father turned

His face away as Jesus bore the weight of our sins. Matthew 27:46 (NLT) records Jesus crying out, "My God, my God, why have you abandoned me?"

Jesus knew loneliness—deeper than we can comprehend. He knew the weight of abandonment, rejection, and despair. And He willingly stepped into that pain for me. For Raymond Smith. He endured all of it so that I could have eternal life, so that Wendy could, and so that you could too.

When Wendy passed, my grief was all-consuming. But the resurrection of Jesus reminded me that death doesn't have the final word. What looked like the end was only the beginning. Just like the Pharisees and Sadducees thought Jesus' story ended at the tomb, Satan may try to convince us that our story ends in loss. But it doesn't. Because of Christ, the tomb is empty—and because of that, our lives are full of hope.

The resurrection is more than an Easter Sunday message— it is the very heartbeat of the Christian faith. Paul reminds us in 1 Corinthians 15:17-20 (NLT), "And if Christ has not been raised, then your faith is useless and you are still guilty of your sins... But in fact, Christ has been raised from the dead. He is the first of a great harvest of all who have died."

Grief presses us to ask difficult questions. But the resurrection answers them with eternal truth. Jesus conquered death, and because He lives, so will we. That truth breathes hope into the darkest places of our lives. It was never clearer to me than when I sat in the pain of Wendy's absence and was reminded that she was more alive now than ever before—in the presence of Jesus.

And if you're walking through grief, I want to ask you something: Do you know that hope? Have you surrendered your life to the One who gave His life for you? Because Jesus didn't just die for Raymond Smith. He died for you. He bore the cross, endured the shame, and rose again so that you could have eternal life.

Romans 10:9 (NLT) declares, "If you openly declare that Jesus is Lord and believe in your heart that God raised him from the dead, you will be saved." That promise is yours. Don't let the weight of grief or the lies of the enemy keep you from the eternal life Christ has offered.

The resurrection means that the story doesn't end at the grave. It means that Wendy's story didn't end at 9:30 PM on April 2, 2024. Because she put her trust in Jesus, her story continues— and so does mine. And so can yours.

If you feel the sting of loneliness, let the resurrection remind you that you are not alone. Jesus is alive. He is with you. He goes before you. And He has prepared a place for you.

Grief may walk beside us, but it does not define us. Loneliness may visit us, but it does not defeat us. The resurrection of Jesus Christ gives us the anchor we need in the storm of loss. It reminds us that the story isn't over—and that the best is yet to come.

As Corrie ten Boom once said, "There is no pit so deep, that God's love is not deeper still."

Hold on to that hope. Lean into the truth of the resurrection. And never forget—because Jesus lives, we live too. Eternity awaits, and in that promise, we find the strength to face another day.

Going Deeper

Loneliness may be one of the most difficult parts of grief. The silence left behind after losing someone we love can feel unbearable. But the resurrection reminds us that death is not the end. Jesus didn't stay in the tomb, and because of that, neither will we. This chapter invited us to see the empty tomb not just as a historical event, but as a personal promise. Let this section help you reflect on how the resurrection can bring hope into your deepest moments of isolation and sorrow.

Scripture Focus:

1 Thessalonians 4:14 (NLT) — "For since we believe that Jesus died and was raised to life again, we also believe that when Jesus returns, God will bring back with him the believers who have died."

Our hope doesn't rest on wishful thinking—it's rooted in the resurrection of Jesus. His victory over death is our assurance that we will be reunited with those who've gone before us.

Reflection Questions:

- How has the resurrection of Christ given you comfort in your grief?
- What does it mean to you that death is not the end of the story?
- Are there moments when you've felt God's presence reminding you of this promise?

Prayer Prompt:
Jesus, thank You for rising from the grave and conquering death. When the loneliness creeps in, remind me that this life is not the end. Help me to hold on to the hope of the resurrection and the reunion that awaits. Anchor me in the truth of Your victory. Amen.

Spiritual Practice:

Take a walk or sit in a quiet space and reflect on the phrase, "Because He lives, I can face tomorrow." Write out what "tomorrow" looks like for you, and how the resurrection gives you strength to keep moving forward.

Janaury 2020 – New York City – Carnegie Hall – Little Big Town Opening Night

Hope in the Resurrection

When shadows fall, and tears appear,
Grief whispers softly, "Hold your fear."
Yet, through the pain, His voice will call,
"Trust in Me—I've conquered all."

The cross, the grave, the empty tomb,
Promise life beyond the gloom.
John 14:1-3 gives peace so sweet,
A place prepared where we'll one day meet.

Though homes feel empty, hours long,
He fills our hearts with faith so strong.
Not dwelling on what we've left behind,
But looking to the hope we'll find.

For in His Word, we see the light,
A home with Him, forever bright.
Revelation shows no more pain,
Through Christ, we'll live again.

So lift your eyes, and trust His plan,
For death is not the final stand.
Hope in the resurrection—pure and true,
Eternal life awaits me and you.

9

Chapter 9: Finding Purpose in Pain

Pain has a way of shifting our perspective. What once seemed secure and predictable can unravel in an instant, leaving behind questions, sorrow, and uncertainty. For me, losing Wendy was that unraveling moment. The grief was consuming. But over time, I began to understand something deeper: that God doesn't waste pain. Instead, He uses it to shape us, guide us, and reveal our purpose in new and unexpected ways.

Before diving into purpose, I want to reflect on something foundational: attitude. Years ago, I had an experience that profoundly shaped my thinking. I was 30 and working at ARCO Oil and Gas. My manager, Greg Gates—ex-military and known for his blunt honesty—sat down with me for my annual performance review. I received a perfect score, but under the feedback section, he had written something that rocked me.

"You're one of the best problem solvers I've ever worked with," he said, "but you're not a team player."

He explained that while I was technically excellent, I preferred to solve problems alone, shutting my office door and isolating myself from the group. He joked that he should hang a sign on my door that said, "Doesn't play well with others."

That feedback was painful—but it was also a gift. It forced me to reflect, to grow, and to change. I began to devour leadership books, starting with John Maxwell's Developing the Leader Within You. I realized that leadership isn't about being the smartest person in the room. It's about collaboration, humility, and communication. One quote that changed my life was from Charles Swindoll: "Life is 10% what happens to me and 90% how I react to it." That quote has hung in every office I've worked in since. Every day, I reminded myself that my attitude is my choice.

That experience helped me grow as a leader, and little did I know, it was preparing me for an even greater trial years later.

There's a reason the Bible speaks of refinement through fire. In 1 Peter 1:7, it says, "These trials will show that your faith is genuine. It is being tested as fire tests and purifies gold..." Just like gold is refined by heat, we are often refined by hardship.

The process is uncomfortable—sometimes excruciating—but the outcome is valuable. Since Wendy's passing, God has been refining me through the fire of grief. That fire pushed me into writing—first my blog and then this book. Both have helped me process my grief while also ministering to others. I believe this is part of the purpose God is shaping from my pain.

I often think of the Prayer of Jabez in 1 Chronicles 4:10, where Jabez asks God to "expand my borders." That's my prayer, too. That God would use this pain to expand my influence—not for my own sake, but so I can reach others who are hurting.

There's another image that's helped me understand the purpose of pain: that of building muscle. Anyone who's ever tried to get stronger knows that muscles only grow when they are pushed, stretched, and even torn. The resistance is what makes them stronger.

Grief has been that resistance for me. But through it, I've been strengthened spiritually. Writing this blog, preparing sermons, and digging into Scripture daily has strengthened my faith in ways I never expected. I'm not just studying God's Word—I'm living it. That's the power of enduring pain with a heart surrendered to God.

Recently, God has made my purpose even clearer. Wendy often told me I should be preaching. Before she became ill, Pastor Max, the pastor at my church, had asked if I'd consider filling in when he was gone. But during her illness, I couldn't even consider it.

Then in February of 2025, I was invited to preach for the first time. I chose Philippians 4—my favorite chapter in the Bible. In April, I preached again, this time on "Building the Bridge to Eternity." Through the pain, God opened a door.

When I preach, my first thought is always, "Would Wendy be proud of this message?" I pour my heart into every sermon, every word written, because I want the pain to have a purpose. I want Satan to lose.

I believe with all my heart that if God woke me up this morning, He's not done with me. I still have work to do. We all do. And the pain we've endured can become the fuel that drives our purpose forward.

The Bible is full of examples of people who found purpose through pain:

- Joseph was betrayed by his brothers, sold into slavery, and wrongfully imprisoned. But through it all, God positioned him to save his family and an entire nation.
- Ruth lost her husband and left everything familiar, but God used her to become the great-grandmother of King David.

· Paul endured beatings, imprisonment, and shipwrecks. Yet he wrote much of the New Testament and helped spread the gospel to the Gentiles.

Their stories show us that pain doesn't disqualify us from purpose. Often, it's the very path that leads us there.

If you're in a season of pain, don't give up. Let God use it. Let Him refine you, strengthen you, and shape you into the person He's calling you to be.

You may not see the full picture yet, but trust that He's working. There is purpose in your pain. And just like Joseph told his brothers in Genesis 50:20, "You intended to harm me, but God intended it all for good. He brought me to this position so I could save the lives of many people."

God has a plan for you, too. Trust Him, lean into the process, and choose every day to live with purpose.

Going Deeper

Pain has a way of either breaking us or shaping us. In this chapter, I shared how God began revealing purpose in the midst of my sorrow—not just through preaching or writing, but in how grief refined and strengthened my faith. If you're still struggling to see purpose in your pain, that's okay. This section isn't meant to force meaning into your suffering but to gently help you explore how God might already be working behind the scenes. Remember, the greater the pain, the greater the potential for redemption.

Scripture Focus:

Romans 8:28 (NLT) — "And we know that God causes everything to work together for the good of those who love God and are called according to his purpose for them."

God never promises a life free from pain, but He does promise to use every part of it for good.

Reflection Questions:

- What are some areas of your life where you've already seen God use pain to produce growth or compassion?
- Are there parts of your story you've been hesitant to share, that could actually help someone else?
- How might your grief become a part of your calling or ministry?

Prayer Prompt:

Father, I don't always understand why things happen the way they do. But I trust You're working even in the pain. Open my eyes to the ways You are shaping me, stretching me, and preparing me for something more. Give me courage to believe that my pain has a purpose, and that You will bring good from it. Amen.

Spiritual Practice:

Write a letter to your future self. Describe the person you hope to become as God continues to use this season to shape you. Seal it in an envelope or tuck it into your Bible. Revisit it in six months or a year and reflect on what God has done.

Learning to make cheese together! Best experience ever!

Purpose in the Pain

Through the valleys, deep and wide,
Pain and grief we cannot hide.
But in the tears, God's promise shines,
A greater purpose, His design.

Romans 8:28, a beacon of light,
In the darkest storm, it holds us tight.
"All things work together," He said,
For those who trust and by Him are led.

Losing loved ones breaks the heart,
But it's not the end; it's just the start.
For in the ashes, purpose grows,
Through every tear, His mercy flows.

Pain refines, it makes us whole,
Strengthening faith, restoring the soul.
In every trial, His love remains,
Turning sorrow into eternal gains.

So hold on to hope, let faith arise,
God's purpose is bigger than what meets the eyes.
Choose gratitude, let joy take flight,
For His promises turn mourning to light.

10

Chapter 10: A Journey Towards Hope

Grief does not come with a roadmap, and there is no one-size-fits-all formula for healing. The chapters of this book have walked through valleys of sorrow, questioned the silence, embraced the comfort of God's presence, and found strength in surrender. We've seen that hope is not the absence of pain but the presence of God in the midst of it.

As this journey draws to a close, the question becomes: where do we go from here?

We press forward with hope.

Hope doesn't mean forgetting. Hope means remembering—with a perspective rooted in eternity. It means looking back on love shared, lessons learned, and lives forever changed—and then lifting our eyes to the future God has promised. This book has emphasized over and over again that our grief is real, our pain is deep, but our God is greater. He sees every tear, hears every cry, and walks with us through every moment of our sorrow.

Hope is not wishful thinking—it's confident expectation in the promises of God. And those promises tell us that death is not the end, that resurrection is real, and that eternity awaits. Because Jesus lives, our loved ones who have trusted Him live too. And one day, we will be reunited, never to be separated again.

As I reflect on the pages of this book and the path that led me here, I realize that this story—this journey—is not just mine. It belongs to everyone who has loved deeply and lost. It belongs to the grieving spouse, the heartbroken parent, the struggling child, the friend who doesn't know how to move forward. This story is for you.

Let me challenge you with this: don't let your grief be the end of your story. Let it be the beginning of something new. Allow God to take the broken pieces and shape them into a purpose. Reflect on what is causing your deepest pain, and then ask God how He can use it. Surrender it to Him—day by day, sometimes hour by hour—and let Him work.

We've talked about finding peace in God's presence, strength in surrender, comfort from others, and eternal hope through the resurrection. But all of this hinges on one vital question: Have you placed your trust in Jesus Christ?

If you haven't, now is the time. Jesus went to the cross for you—not just to save you from sin but to give you hope in this life and the next. His resurrection guarantees that death is not final, and His love assures you that you are never alone. Romans 10:9 (NLT) says, "If you openly declare that Jesus is Lord and believe in your heart that God raised him from the dead, you will be saved."

Surrender to Him today. Let the hope we've talked about in this book become your own.

As we come to the close of this journey together, I want to leave you with the verse that brought me the most comfort during my darkest nights. A verse that reminded me that even though grief walks beside me for a season, it will not follow me into eternity. That verse is Revelation 21:4 (NLT):

"He will wipe every tear from their eyes, and there will be no more death or sorrow or crying or pain. All these things are gone forever."

Let those last five words sink in—"All these things are gone forever."

No more death.

No more sorrow.

No more pain.

No more grief.

No more wondering how to take the next step.

No more lonely nights or tear-stained pillows.

Gone. Forever.

This verse brought me deep peace, not only because of the beauty it describes, but because of what it told me about Wendy. She is no longer in pain. She is no longer wasting away. She can eat whatever she wants now—free, joyful, radiant in the presence of her Savior. And one day, I'll join her. We'll walk together again, without fear of saying goodbye.

This promise doesn't remove the pain of grief, but it reframes it. It anchors it in something eternal. It reminds me that there will be no more goodbyes, no more caskets, no more phone calls bearing unbearable news. In Heaven, there is only reunion, only life, only love. That's what we're promised through Jesus Christ.

So if you're weary—if the weight of grief feels too heavy, if you're clinging by a thread—I want you to know this: God sees you. God loves you. And God has promised that the tears you're crying now will one day be wiped away by His own hand.

And if you've never fully surrendered your heart to Christ—if you're wondering how to know for sure that this promise is for you— it is as easy as A-B-C. Admit you are a sinner in need of a Savior. Believe that Christ died on the cross to pay for your sins and He rose on the third day. Confess with your mouth He is Lord. Because these promises aren't just beautiful—they're eternal. And they are available to all who place their trust in Jesus.

Going Deeper

This final chapter is not an ending—it's a beginning. You've walked through the sorrow, wrestled with the questions, and opened your heart to hope. You may not have all the answers, and that's okay. What matters is that you've kept walking. This final reflection isn't about looking back—it's about stepping forward into whatever God has for you next.

Scripture Focus:

Philippians 3:13–14 (NLT) — "But I focus on this one thing: Forgetting the past and looking forward to what lies ahead, I press on to reach the end of the race and receive the heavenly prize..."

You may carry grief, but you do not walk without purpose. There's still a race to run—and God is with you every step of the way.

Guided Reflection:

- What has God revealed to you through this grief journey?
- What do you want to carry forward from this season?
- What is one small step you can take today to live with purpose?

Prayer Prompt:

Lord, thank You for walking with me through the darkness. As I move forward, I ask for Your guidance, strength, and clarity. Use my story to bring hope to others. Help me to live with boldness, rooted in the eternal hope You've promised. Amen.

Commissioning Challenge:

Write down one act of courage you'll commit to this week—whether it's reaching out to someone, telling part of your story, or simply spending quiet time with God. Keep it visible. Let it remind you: grief may shape you, but it doesn't define you. Hope does.

A Closing Prayer of Hope

Heavenly Father,

Thank You for being the God who sees every tear and understands every ache in our hearts. Thank You for sending Jesus, not just to walk this broken world, but to conquer sin, death, and grief itself. Thank You for the hope of eternity.

We rest in Your promise that one day You will wipe every tear from our eyes—and that all these things will be gone forever. Until then, help us walk in the light of that promise. Let it give us strength when we're weak, joy when we feel empty, and peace when we feel alone.

For every person reading these words, I ask You to fill them with the hope of Heaven. Give them glimpses of Your grace today and confidence in the eternity You have promised. May they live each day with the expectation of glory and the comfort of knowing that You are with them, now and forever.

In the mighty name of Jesus,
Amen.

A Word Before the Poem

As I come to the close of this book, it's been just over a year since Wendy went home to be with the Lord. Writing and editing these pages has been one of the most difficult yet meaningful experiences of my life. In full honesty, I delayed finishing the final edits for over three months—because doing so meant facing the reality of our journey one more time.

This poem reflects the path I've walked—through loss, through the ache of loneliness, and into the quiet, steady light of eternal hope. My prayer is that as you read it, you will not only feel seen and understood but that you will also be reminded: there is indeed hope beyond the tears.

Hope Beyond the Tears

I woke to silence louder than sound,
   A house too still, a world unbound.
   The coffee didn't brew, but grief did rise—
   A life once full now grieved through cries.

Loneliness lingered in each empty room,
   Darkness hung thick, a relentless gloom.
   I called to the echoes, but none replied,
   Just memories soft and tears I'd cried.

Why, O Lord? The question screamed,
   This isn't the life that we had dreamed.
   You could have stopped it, changed the end—
   Not taken my love, my heart, my friend.

But as I wept in sacred despair,
   I sensed a whisper in the air.
   "I know your pain, your loss, your strife—
   I gave My Son to give you life."

And suddenly the silence stirred,
   By promises found within God's Word.
   That death is not the closing part—
   But the door through which new hope will start.

I saw the cross and empty grave,
   Proof of the love that came to save.
   He walked through death, alone, betrayed—
   So I'd have hope when skies turned gray.

Each morning brought another test,
    But God walked with me through the rest.
    And little hands that reached for mine,
    Reminded me His grace is kind.

My niece, in tears, had spilled her drink,
    Embarrassed, small, right on the brink.
    She asked for me—her Uncle's care—
    Not knowing I needed her right there.

God's comfort came in subtle ways,
    In laughter shared, in hugs, in praise.
    He sent me people, warm and near,
    To remind me that He's always here.

Now every tear and every ache,
    Is not in vain or some mistake.
    Through brokenness, a purpose grows,
    A deeper faith, a love that shows.

I preach, I write, I testify,
    That hope lives on, it will not die.
    For though she's gone from earthly view,
    God's not done with me—or you.

This book, this path, these pages turned,
    Are soaked in truth and lessons learned.
    The greater the love, the grief more deep—
    But greater still the hope I keep.

So when you cry and feel alone,

Remember this: you're not your own.
God weeps with you, walks every mile,
And one day, tears give way to smile.

For in that place beyond the skies,
  Where no more pain or sorrow lies—
  We'll meet again, all whole, all healed—
By promises God has revealed.

And what was broken will be restored,
  By mercy great and grace outpoured.
  Until that day, I'll live and say—
  There's hope beyond the tears we pray.

A Final Reflection

As I was finishing the final edits of this book, I took time to read through the poem, *Hope Beyond the Tears*, one more time. Outside my window in Farmers Valley, the world was wrapped in a quiet snowfall—gray skies, bare trees, and stillness that echoed the weight of grief. As I reached the final stanza, reflecting on eternity and the hope that shines beyond sorrow, something remarkable happened.

The sun broke through the clouds.

Golden rays pierced the heavy sky, lighting up the snowy landscape with breathtaking brilliance. It felt as though God Himself was reminding me that grief, like winter, may linger— but hope always rises. That moment became a vivid picture of what this entire journey has taught me: the days may be heavy, the pain real, but God's promises are brighter than any storm.

Hope is not the absence of sorrow—it is the presence of His light in the midst of it.

July 3, 2019 - Wendy's Birthday - Finger Lakes - New York

11

Chapter 11: A Tribute

Harvesting Pumpkins – Another one of Wendy's Favorite Times of the Year

April 2, 2025 marked one year that Wendy had been in Heaven. I didn't want to write some pity filled Facebook post that drew attention to me. I decided I would write a tribute to my wife.

A Life Well-Loved — My Tribute to Wendy
April 2, One Year in Heaven

She walked in grace, with hands that healed,
A heart for truth, a love revealed.
With every lesson she would teach,
She lived the faith she sought to preach.

Her prayers were quiet, strong, and deep,
She sowed in tears what we now reap.
For every child and kin she knew,
She battled on her knees for you.

A wife, a friend, a love so true,
She made the house a home for two.
With every plate and flowered bed,
She wrapped our hearts in all she did.

Her laughter warmed the coldest day,
Her smile could chase the dark away.
She gave with joy, she lived with light,
A beacon burning ever bright.

But don't you mourn for her today,
She wouldn't have it be that way.
For she has reached her final goal—
The Savior's arms, her heart made whole.

She walks now where the angels sing,

Beside the throne, beside her King.
With loved ones past, now face to face,
   She basks in everlasting grace.

   Yet still, her legacy lives on,
  In every life she touched and shone.
  A teacher, servant, sister, bride—
She lived her faith, a light that shined.

So we'll not weep for what is gone,
But thank the Lord for what lived on.
For Wendy's life was Heaven-tied,
And now she lives—just glorified.

12

Appendix: Stories of Grief and Comfort in the Bible

Each of these accounts reveals a God who sees, hears, and responds to the brokenhearted. Included are brief synopses so that you can understand each story at a glance and consider how God's comfort and presence are demonstrated throughout Scripture.

1. Job: Loss and Restoration
Key Scripture: Job 1–2, Job 42:10–17
Synopsis: Job was a righteous man who lost everything—his children, wealth, and health—due to a test of his faith. Despite intense grief and confusion, he refused to curse God. Job's friends misunderstood his suffering, but God never abandoned him. In the end, Job's fortunes were restored, and he received even greater blessings.
Comfort Principle: God honors steadfast faith and walks with us even in silence.

2. David: Mourning and Consolation

Key Scripture: 2 Samuel 12:15–23

Synopsis: After committing grievous sins, David's child became ill and eventually died. David fasted and prayed while the child was sick but worshiped God once the child passed away, demonstrating a heart submitted to God's will. This moment showed David's deep grief, his trust in God, and his hope of reunion in eternity.

Comfort Principle: Grief is honest and raw, but worship leads us to healing.

3. Naomi and Ruth: Shared Loss, Shared Hope

Key Scripture: Ruth 1–4

Synopsis: Naomi lost her husband and two sons while living in a foreign land. Her grief turned into bitterness as she returned home, feeling empty. But her daughter-in-law Ruth stayed with her, and through God's providence, Ruth married Boaz and gave Naomi a grandson, continuing her family's legacy.

Comfort Principle: God brings hope from brokenness and uses others to walk with us.

4. Mary and Martha: Jesus Wept Too

Key Scripture: John 11:1–44

Synopsis: When Lazarus died, his sisters Mary and Martha mourned deeply. Jesus came and wept with them, even though He knew He would raise Lazarus from the dead. His tears revealed His compassion and the depth of His love for those who grieve.

Comfort Principle: Jesus enters into our grief and brings resurrection hope.

5. Hannah: Grief in Waiting

Key Scripture: 1 Samuel 1:1–20

Synopsis: Hannah endured years of infertility and the mocking of others. In her anguish, she poured out her heart to God in prayer. God heard her cry and eventually gave her a son, Samuel, whom she dedicated to the Lord.

Comfort Principle: God hears the prayers of the brokenhearted.

6. Jesus: The Garden and the Cross

Key Scripture: Luke 22:39–46; Matthew 27:45–46

Synopsis: In Gethsemane, Jesus grieved the suffering that awaited Him and prayed in anguish. On the cross, He cried out in apparent abandonment. He bore the weight of humanity's sin, experiencing the ultimate loneliness so that we would never be alone.

Comfort Principle: We are never truly alone—Jesus understands our pain.

7. Paul: The Thorn and the Grace

Key Scripture: 2 Corinthians 12:7–10

Synopsis: Paul pleaded with God to remove a persistent struggle, which he called a "thorn in the flesh." God did not remove it but instead promised that His grace would be sufficient. Paul came to understand that his weakness allowed God's strength to be made perfect.

Comfort Principle: Sometimes comfort comes not in change, but in strength to endure.

13

When You Need More Help: Reaching Out for Support

Grief is a journey that looks different for everyone. Some find comfort and healing through time, scripture, prayer, and community. Others may feel stuck—unable to move forward despite their best efforts. If that's you, please know this: you are not alone, and there is no shame in seeking additional help.

God designed us for community. While His Word brings comfort, sometimes we also need someone to walk with us through our darkest valleys. A trained Christian grief counselor can help you process your pain, offer biblical encouragement, and guide you toward healing.

Start with Your Church

If you are part of a local church, ask your pastor or church leadership if they offer grief counseling or support groups. Many churches have trained counselors or lay leaders who are equipped to help. Simply starting the conversation with someone you trust in your church can be a powerful first step.

Online Christian Grief Counseling Resources

If in-person support isn't available or you prefer online options, several faith-based services offer grief counseling and support virtually:

- **Grief Share**

Website: https://www.griefshare.org/
GriefShare offers local and online group support grounded in biblical principles. It's one of the most trusted Christian grief support networks.

- **Better Help**

Website: https://www.betterhelp.com
A professional Christian counseling service available online. You can be matched with a licensed therapist who shares your faith.

- **Focus on the Family Counseling Services**

Website: https://www.focusonthefamily.com/get-help/counseling-services-and-referrals/
Offers one-time complimentary consultations and can help connect you with a Christian counselor in your area.

- **Biblical Counseling Coalition**

Website: https://www.biblicalcounselingcoalition.org/
A network of biblical counselors and resources that can help

you locate certified Christian counselors near you.

You Don't Have to Walk Alone

Sometimes grief can feel like a fog that never lifts. But I want to encourage you with this truth—God sees you. He understands your sorrow, and He's placed people in this world to help. Reaching out isn't a sign of weakness; it's a step of courage and faith.

Your healing matters. Don't be afraid to ask for help when you need it. And always remember: the God of all comfort walks with you—every step of the way.

14

Cited Quotes and Sayings

Chapter 3 – When Love Meets Loss

- *"Grief is the price we pay for love."*

— **Queen Elizabeth II**, following the death of her husband Prince Philip in 2021.

Chapter 5 – Finding Strength in Surrender

- *"Life is 10% what happens to me and 90% how I react to it."*

— **Charles R. Swindoll**, American pastor and author.

Chapter 7 – Holding on to Eternal Hope

- *"Never be afraid to trust an unknown future to a known God."*

— **Corrie ten Boom**, Dutch Christian who helped Jews escape the Nazis during WWII.

Chapter 8 – Hope in the Resurrection

- *"There is no pit so deep, that God's love is not deeper still."*

— **Corrie ten Boom**, from her book *The Hiding Place*.

15

30-Day Prayer Journal for the Grieving Heart

Grief is a journey, and prayer can be the lifeline that keeps us connected to God through the darkest moments. This 30-day journal is designed to walk with you through the ups and downs of grief. Each day features a guiding question or theme, a Scripture from the New Living Translation (NLT), a short reflection, and a prayer prompt. You are encouraged to reflect, journal your thoughts, and be honest with God—He is big enough to handle your questions, tears, and fears.

Day 1 – Where Is God in My Grief?

- Scripture: Psalm 34:18 (NLT) – "The Lord is close to the brokenhearted; he rescues those whose spirits are crushed."
- Reflection: In the pain of loss, it can feel like God is distant. But Scripture reminds us that He draws near to the brokenhearted.
- Prayer Prompt: Ask God to make His presence known even in your sorrow. Tell Him how you feel today.

Day 2 – Why Did This Happen?

- Scripture: Isaiah 55:8-9 (NLT) – "'My thoughts are nothing like your thoughts,' says the Lord. 'And my ways are far beyond anything you could imagine.'"
- Reflection: We may never understand the "why," but God asks us to trust that His ways are higher.
- Prayer Prompt: Share your "why" questions with God. Then ask for peace beyond your understanding.

Day 3 – What Does It Mean to Grieve With Hope?

- Scripture: 1 Thessalonians 4:13 (NLT) – "And now, dear brothers and sisters, we want you to know what will happen to the believers who have died so you will not grieve like people who have no hope."
- Reflection: Grief with hope acknowledges the pain but clings to the promise of eternal life.
- Prayer Prompt: Thank God for the hope you have in Christ. Ask Him to strengthen your faith today.

Day 4 – When the Silence Is Loud

- Scripture: Lamentations 3:25-26 (NLT) – "The Lord is good to those who depend on him, to those who search for him. So it is good to wait quietly for salvation from the Lord."
- Reflection: Silence can be painful, but sometimes it is in the silence that God speaks the loudest.
- Prayer Prompt: Sit in silence with God. Invite Him into that space.

Day 5 – Learning to Surrender

- Scripture: Matthew 11:28-29 (NLT) – "Come to me, all of you who are weary and carry heavy burdens, and I will give you rest. Take my yoke upon you. Let me teach you, because I am humble and gentle at heart, and you will find rest for your souls."
- Reflection: True comfort is found when we surrender our heavy burdens to Christ.
- Prayer Prompt: Tell God what burden you're holding onto. Ask Him to carry it for you.

Day 6 – When the Tears Won't Stop

- Scripture: Psalm 56:8 (NLT) – "You keep track of all my sorrows. You have collected all my tears in your bottle. You have recorded each one in your book."
- Reflection: God sees your tears. None of them are wasted.
- Prayer Prompt: Thank God for seeing your sorrow. Share your heart with Him today.

Day 7 – Finding Purpose in the Pain

- Scripture: Romans 8:28 (NLT) – "And we know that God causes everything to work together for the good of those who love God and are called according to his purpose for them."
- Reflection: God can redeem even the deepest pain for a greater purpose.
- Prayer Prompt: Ask God to begin showing you glimpses of purpose in your grief.

Day 8 – The Battle for Your Mind

- Scripture: Philippians 4:8 (NLT) – "Fix your thoughts on what is true, and honorable, and right, and pure, and lovely, and admirable. Think about things that are excellent and worthy of praise."
- Reflection: Your mind is a battleground. Focus it on God's truth.
- Prayer Prompt: Ask God to help you take every thought captive and focus on His promises.

Day 9 – God's Peace Is Different

- Scripture: John 14:27 (NLT) – "I am leaving you with a gift— peace of mind and heart. And the peace I give is a gift the world cannot give. So don't be troubled or afraid."
- Reflection: God's peace is not circumstantial. It's a divine gift.
- Prayer Prompt: Ask God to fill your heart and mind with His peace today.

Day 10 – When You Feel Alone

- Scripture: Hebrews 13:5b (NLT) – "For God has said, 'I will never fail you. I will never abandon you.'"
- Reflection: God's presence doesn't leave just because people do.
- Prayer Prompt: Invite God into your loneliness. Ask Him to be your companion today.

Day 11: Strength to Keep Going

- Scripture: Isaiah 40:31 (NLT) – "But those who trust in the Lord will find new strength."
- Reflection: God will renew your strength day by day.
- Prayer Prompt: Pray for strength to face this day and each day ahead.

Day 12: When Tears Won't Stop

- Scripture: Psalm 56:8 (NLT) – "You keep track of all my sorrows. You have collected all my tears in your bottle."
- Reflection: God sees every tear. He remembers.
- Prayer Prompt: Pour out your emotions to God. He welcomes them.

Day 13: Trusting Again

- Scripture: Proverbs 3:5-6 (NLT) – "Trust in the Lord with all your heart... He will show you which path to take."
- Reflection: Trust grows as you lean on God, step by step.
- Prayer Prompt: Ask God to help you trust Him more fully.

Day 14: Letting Go of Guilt

- Scripture: 1 John 1:9 (NLT) – "If we confess our sins... he is faithful and just to forgive us."
- Reflection: Guilt is a burden God never asked you to carry.
- Prayer Prompt: Confess any lingering guilt and receive God's forgiveness.

Day 15: God's Nearness in the Night

- Scripture: Psalm 121:3-4 (NLT) – "He never slumbers or sleeps."
- Reflection: When you can't sleep, God is still awake, still with you.
- Prayer Prompt: Ask God to fill your sleepless hours with His peace.

Day 16: Light in the Darkness

- Scripture: John 1:5 (NLT) – "The light shines in the darkness, and the darkness can never extinguish it."
- Reflection: Darkness cannot overcome Christ's light.
- Prayer Prompt: Ask God to shine His light in the darkest corners of your grief.

Day 17: Freedom from Fear

- Scripture: 2 Timothy 1:7 (NLT) – "For God has not given us a spirit of fear... but of power, love, and self-discipline."
- Reflection: Fear doesn't have the final word.
- Prayer Prompt: Ask God to replace your fear with His courage.

Day 18: Finding Joy Again

- Scripture: Psalm 30:5 (NLT) – "Weeping may last through the night, but joy comes with the morning."
- Reflection: Joy will return. It always does with God.
- Prayer Prompt: Ask God to restore joy to your spirit.

Day 19: Healing Takes Time

- Scripture: Ecclesiastes 3:1,4 (NLT) – "For everything there is a season... a time to cry and a time to laugh."
- Reflection: Give yourself grace. Healing is not rushed.
- Prayer Prompt: Pray for patience as you walk your unique path of healing.

Day 20: God Understands Grief

- Scripture: John 11:35 (NLT) – "Then Jesus wept."
- Reflection: Jesus knows your sorrow firsthand.
- Prayer Prompt: Invite Jesus to sit with you in your grief.

Day 21 – When You Feel Weak

- Scripture: "Each time he said, 'My grace is all you need. My power works best in weakness.' So now I am glad to boast about my weaknesses, so that the power of Christ can work through me." – 2 Corinthians 12:9 (NLT)
- Reflection Prompt: What areas of your life feel especially difficult right now? How can you rely more on God's strength today?
- Prayer Prompt: Ask God to meet you in your weakness and fill you with His strength and grace.

Day 22 – Trusting God's Timing

- Scripture: "For everything there is a season, a time for every activity under heaven." – Ecclesiastes 3:1 (NLT)
- Reflection Prompt: Are you struggling with how long your grief has lasted? What would it look like to surrender your timeline to God?

- Prayer Prompt: Pray for patience and trust in God's perfect timing.

Day 23 – Finding Joy Again

- Scripture: "Weeping may last through the night, but joy comes with the morning." – Psalm 30:5b (NLT)
- Reflection Prompt: Have you had moments of joy during your grief? How did those moments feel?
- Prayer Prompt: Thank God for any glimpses of joy and ask Him to help you continue finding joy in His presence.

Day 24 – Comforting Others

- Scripture: "He comforts us in all our troubles so that we can comfort others." – 2 Corinthians 1:4a (NLT)
- Reflection Prompt: Who in your life may need comfort today? How has your grief journey prepared you to help someone else?
- Prayer Prompt: Ask God to use your pain to minister to others and bring healing to those around you.

Day 25 – Embracing Hope

- Scripture: "I pray that God, the source of hope, will fill you completely with joy and peace because you trust in him." – Romans 15:13 (NLT)
- Reflection Prompt: What does hope look like to you right now? Where are you placing your hope today?
- Prayer Prompt: Pray for a heart full of hope, peace, and joy that overflows to others.

Day 26 – God Is With You

- Scripture: "The Lord himself goes before you and will be with you; he will never leave you nor forsake you." – Deuteronomy 31:8 (NLT)
- Reflection Prompt: When have you most felt God's presence during this season of grief?
- Prayer Prompt: Thank God for going before you and staying with you. Invite Him into today's journey.

Day 27 – The Power of Prayer

- Scripture: "The earnest prayer of a righteous person has great power and produces wonderful results." – James 5:16b (NLT)
- Reflection Prompt: How has prayer helped you during your grief? Is it something you've struggled with?
- Prayer Prompt: Ask God to deepen your prayer life and help you see His responses even in small ways.

Day 28 – Letting Go of Guilt

- Scripture: "So now there is no condemnation for those who belong to Christ Jesus." – Romans 8:1 (NLT)
- Reflection Prompt: Are you carrying any guilt from your loved one's passing? What truth from Scripture speaks against that guilt?
- Prayer Prompt: Ask God to remove guilt and replace it with peace, knowing you are forgiven and free in Christ.

Day 29 – Living with Purpose

- Scripture: "For we are God's masterpiece. He has created us anew in Christ Jesus, so we can do the good things he planned for us long ago." – Ephesians 2:10 (NLT)
- Reflection Prompt: How is God revealing your purpose through grief? What good works is He preparing you to walk in?
- Prayer Prompt: Pray for clarity, courage, and direction as you seek to live purposefully even through pain.

Day 30 – Looking Toward Heaven

- Scripture: "'He will wipe every tear from their eyes, and there will be no more death or sorrow or crying or pain. All these things are gone forever.'" – Revelation 21:4 (NLT)
- Reflection Prompt: How does the promise of Heaven encourage you today? What are you most looking forward to in eternity?
- Prayer Prompt: Thank God for the eternal hope you have in Christ. Rejoice in the promise of Heaven where grief is no more.

Take your time with this journal. Revisit days as needed. Use the space to reflect, write, and cry if you need to. God meets us in our grief with gentleness, and He is faithful to heal our hearts day by day.

About Disciple Blueprint

Disciple Blueprint, www.discipleblueprint.com is a ministry dedicated to helping Christians grow in their faith and live out their calling as disciples of Christ. Founded by Raymond Smith, the mission of Disciple Blueprint is to provide practical resources, Bible studies, and personal reflections that equip believers to deepen their relationship with God and share His love with others.

Through insightful blog posts, downloadable tools, and teaching aids, Disciple Blueprint offers encouragement and guidance for every stage of the Christian journey. Whether you are a new believer seeking foundational truths, a seasoned Christian exploring deeper discipleship, or someone looking to teach and lead others in their faith, you will find valuable resources to support your walk with Christ.

Key topics covered on Disciple Blueprint include:

- Bible study methods and tools
- Practical guidance for Christian living
- Navigating grief and life's challenges with faith
- Discipleship strategies for individuals and groups
- Family resources to help parents and guardians teach their children about God

At Disciple Blueprint, our goal is to inspire you to live boldly for

Christ, embrace your unique calling, and grow in love, humility, and service. We believe that God's Word has the power to transform lives, and we are committed to helping you discover His truths in a meaningful and accessible way.

To explore more, visit www.discipleblueprint.com and join our growing community. By subscribing to our newsletter, you'll receive regular updates, exclusive resources, and encouragement to help you stay rooted in your faith.

Together, let's pursue the life Christ has called us to live—a life of love, service, and unwavering faith.

About the Author

Raymond Smith is a follower of Christ, a storyteller, and someone who has walked the long road of grief—and found hope on the other side. After a 33-year marriage to his beloved wife, Wendy, Raymond faced one of the most difficult seasons of his life. This book was born out of that pain and out of his desire to help others find comfort in Christ.

With over four decades of leadership experience in the IT world, Raymond brings clarity, humility, and insight to everything he writes. Now retired from corporate life, he has dedicated himself to ministry through writing, teaching, and speaking. He is the founder of *Disciple Blueprint*, a Christian blog committed to helping believers grow in their faith through Bible study and practical discipleship. Raymond will be launching the Disciple Blueprint Podcast soon.

Raymond serves at Hilltop Baptist Church in Northwest Pennsylvania, where he occasionally preaches and actively supports his local church family. He is also a proud uncle who finds deep joy and healing through time with his niece and nephews.

When he's not writing or preparing to teach, you'll find him sitting on the front porch with his dogs, watching the hills of Farmers Valley, or cheering on his favorite sports teams.

You can find more of Raymond's writing at:
  www.discipleblueprint.com

Or email him at: raymond@discipleblueprint.com

You can connect with me on:
- https://www.discipleblueprint.com
- https://x.com/Dblueblog
- https://www.facebook.com/discipleblueprint
- https://www.instagram.com/discipleblueprint

Subscribe to my newsletter:
- https://discipleblueprint.com/?ff_landing=4

www.ingramcontent.com/pod-product-compliance
Lightning Source LLC
Chambersburg PA
CBHW071528120626
46550CB00006B/2391

*9 7 9 8 9 9 9 8 5 6 8 6 3 3 *